PERFORMANCE EDITIONS

LISZT

CONSOLATIONS and LIEBESTRAUME

Edited and Recorded by Alexandre Dossin

To access companion recorded performances online, visit:
www.halleonard.com/mylibrary

Enter Code
2331-3884-2898-9075

On the cover:
The Town and Lake Como
by Jean Baptiste Camille Corot
(1796–1875)

ISBN 978-1-6177-4229-3

G. SCHIRMER, Inc.

DISTRIBUTED BY

HAL•LEONARD®
CORPORATION
7777 W. BLUEMOUND RD. P.O. BOX 13819 MILWAUKEE, WI 53213

www.musicsalesclassical.com
www.halleonard.com

CONTENTS

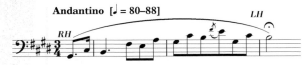

The price of this publication includes access to companion recorded performances online, for download or streaming, using the unique code found on the title page. Visit **www.halleonard.com/mylibrary** and enter the access code.

HISTORICAL NOTES

FRANZ LISZT (1811-1886)

Arguably the best pianist of all times, Franz Liszt composed much piano and orchestral music. Liszt lived from 1811 until 1886, and in his long and productive life created immortal works such as the Piano Sonata in B minor, a popular series of Symphonic Poems, exciting piano concertos and an incredible amount of solo piano music. Born in Raiding (located in Austria, part of Hungary at the time), he showed great talent at the piano from an early age and soon became one of the most celebrated child prodigies since Mozart. When looking at his schedule of performances during the years of concert touring, starting with his first world tour in 1823 and ending with his last performance in 1847, one can only be amazed by the distances covered in those years of horse-carriage travel. In a surprising move, Liszt decided to retire from that itinerant life at the age of 35—his last official public performance was in September of 1847, in Elisabetgrad (Ukraine)—and started a very productive teaching, conducting and composing career.

Even though Liszt is often mostly known by his virtuosic piano works, his contribution to the musical world went far beyond that of a composer of "show-pieces." The majority of early works, written prior to 1848, are indeed very showy and at times display a very simple musical language. However, the move to Weimar in 1848 changed that in a deep way, and his musical output in the post-Weimar period is much less dependent on brilliant pianistic tricks; indeed, many scholars agree that his music became in many ways influential to future composers. This change in his compositional style is easy to prove by analyzing the numerous revisions of early piano works: as a rule, textures became less complicated, and Liszt was able to get better results with less

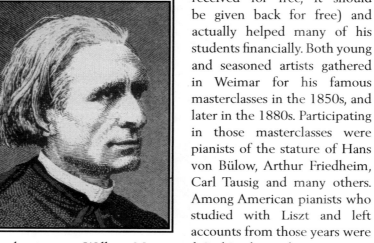

work. Obvious examples of such revisions are the Transcendental Etudes and the Paganini Etudes. Both exist in pre- and post-Weimar versions; a quick glance at the scores shows the pianistic changes, and for this reason the revised versions are the ones commonly performed nowadays.

Liszt was also one of the first great "Master Teachers" and the creator of the piano masterclasses that we know today. He never charged for lessons (his motto was "Génie oblige!" if one had a talent, received for free, it should be given back for free) and actually helped many of his students financially. Both young and seasoned artists gathered in Weimar for his famous masterclasses in the 1850s, and later in the 1880s. Participating in those masterclasses were pianists of the stature of Hans von Bülow, Arthur Friedheim, Carl Tausig and many others. Among American pianists who studied with Liszt and left accounts from those years were William Mason and Carl Lachmund.

As a conductor, Liszt was always keen to present new works and was happy to lend his prestige to young composers. Liszt was one of the active participants of what historians and scholars came to call the "War of the Romantics:" an exciting musical battle between the "old" school (Brahms, Schumann, Mendelssohn and the Leipzig Conservatory) and the "new" school (Liszt, Berlioz and Wagner). As described by Alan Walker, this intellectual and esthetic conflict happened "when a number of great ideas vied with one another for the allegiance of musicians everywhere: programme music versus absolute music, form versus content, the oneness versus the separateness of the arts, newness versus oldness, revolution versus reaction" (Walker, *The Weimar Years*, p. 338).

PERFORMANCE NOTES

Liszt's Piano Music

Fingering

Fingerings are editorial and have in mind a medium-sized hand. Some adjustments may be needed for smaller hands. As a rule, fingerings were carefully chosen to convey the phrasing and articulation, not simply for comfort. Two numbers connected by a hyphen represent a slide between black and white keys; two numbers connected by a slur represent finger substitution. In some cases, an optional fingering is shown below or above in parenthesis.

Pedaling

It is practically impossible to notate pedaling in an effective way. Good pedaling depends on many variables (quality of the instrument, performer's touch, how far the pedal is pressed, specific acoustics, etc.), that any effort becomes almost pointless, since the performer will need to make the final decisions, using his or her musical abilities and sensibilities. Therefore, pedal indications are only suggestions, with the final decision left to the performer, based on specifics of the instrument and the concert hall. In the sections where effective pedaling is almost impossible to notate or too obvious, it is omitted altogether. Except for instances where a special sound effect is needed, good pedaling is not supposed to be heard. In other words, use the pedal in such a way so the textures are always clear and not compromised by excessive blurring. The indication *no ped* means: use as little pedal as possible – usually in very light, staccato textures.

Metronome markings

Metronome markings are editorial. Instead of suggesting a specific marking, a small range of possible tempos is provided. Performances outside those markings may lack the necessary clarity if too fast or may not allow for correct phrasing if too slow.

Dynamics and Articulation

Dynamics and articulations are Liszt's throughout.

Notes on the Individual Movements

Consolations

Until 1992, there was only one available published version of the Consolations, a set of six pensive pieces published in 1850. In 1992, Henle published for the first time an early version of the Consolations, edited by eminent musicologists Maria Eckhardt and Ernst-Günter Heinemann. This early version differs from the commonly published set of Consolations: in general, the texture is more elaborate in the early version, and the third piece is a completely different work, not the famous D-flat Major *Lento placido* that became an encore piece for numerous artists. The present edition includes only the familiar version and is based on the 1850 Breitkopf & Härtel edition (Leipzig). Other editions consulted were Henle (Maria Echkardt and Ernst-Günter Heinemann, editors, 1992), Schirmer (Schirmer's Library of Musical Classics, vol. 341, 1895/1915, Rafael Joseffy, editor), Schott (August Schmid-Lindner, editor, 1953), Durand (L. Garban, editor, 1927) and Editio Musica Budapest (Imre Sulyok and Imre Mezo, editors, 1981).

The origins of the title are not certain. Searle, Sulyok and Mezo affirm that it comes from Sainte-Beuve poems (Searle, p. 61). While Eckhardt and Heinemann, mention the Sainte-Beuve poems as a possibility, they consider that less likely than a possible Lamartine inspiration, more specifically his poem "Une larme, ou Consolation" (Henle Edition no. 465, Preface). The set of six short, slow pieces is definitely quiet and "consoling," thus the title can be considered very appropriate. There is a predominance of E Major (4 pieces are in this key), with two of the pieces written in D-Flat Major. Despite the fact that No. 3 became disproportionally more famous than its counterparts, this set definitely works well together and should be performed more often as such, with a feeling of almost "attacca" between some of the individual pieces.

Consolation No. 1

Only 25 measures long, this is the shortest of the group and according to Lina Ramann's *Liszt-Pädagogium*, based on Liszt's masterclasses, it should proceed to the second piece without a break. The texture is not purely pianistic; one could easily imagine this being played by a string quartet. All parts of the chords are important, but one can obtain a better sound quality by voicing the outer parts more intensely. Beginning in m. 8, the first violin takes the lead with poignant melodic material in G-sharp minor. Use arm-weight to bring out this melody, while keeping the accompanying chords expressive but soft. The appoggiatura in m. 13 marks the arrival of G Major and with it a very special color in this piece. This appoggiatura should be played on the beat, as an eight-note, with the half-note becoming a dotted quarter note. This is the culminating point of this miniature and it should be played with great expression and sensitivity.

Consolation No. 2

The incomplete measure that ends No. 1 is completed by the pick-up quarter note in this piece. According to Ramann, the metronome markings of the first and second piece are, respectively, 54 for the half-note and 126 for the quarter. This is in line with the indication Un poco più mosso for No. 2. This is a more fluid texture, with the main melodic material in the right hand being accompanied by an undulating, arpeggiated left-hand figuration. The two layers should be well-defined, using arm weight for the melody (*cantando espressivo*, as suggested by Liszt) combined with very supple wrist and fingers in the left hand. In the section from mm. 38–45, practice playing the melody with separate hands, without the other two layers (bass and arpeggios). Make sure the sound between the hands match.

Consolation No. 3

This is by far the most famous and often performed piece from this set. Because of its key and overall texture similarities to Chopin's Nocturne Op. 27, No. 2, it is sometimes considered by scholars an homage to Chopin after his death in 1849 (Eckhardt and Heinemann). The main challenge of this piece is keeping the low D-flat sounding for a long time, as the sustain pedal is changed. On our modern pianos, this can be accomplished by the sostenuto pedal. I suggest playing the low D-flat with the right hand (2nd or 3rd fingers), while the left hand is kept positioned with the arpeggio figuration. Depending on the instrument, the low D-flat may be played again, softly, if the sound dies too quickly. One could say that this piece has only one challenge, but a very important

one: keeping the three layers very distinct. The undulating accompaniment should never become too present, and the bass notes should give the melody room to blossom. In Liszt' words: "play the triplets in No. 3 somewhat freely and indeed do not put too much stress on the quarter note beat" (Gölerich Diary Notes, p. 69).

Consolation No. 4

Sometimes referred to as Stern-Consolation because of the guiding star printed in some editions, the melody for this piece was provided by the grand duchess of Weimar Maria Pawlowna, the sister of Tsar Nicholas I of Russia. This piece is also in D-flat Major, but returns to a more chordal, hymnal character. There are conflicting indications regarding the placement of hands in measures 25–27: Ramann indicates that Liszt said "No hand crossing! – the melody is to be carried on by the right hand" (EMB edition, Z. 12 697, p. 9). On the other side, we read in the Göllerich Diary Notes an entry mentioning a performance of the Consolations, with the following annotation:

> The master played all themes himself. It was magnificent! During No. ? he stressed that at the passage where the theme comes in the bass when the hands cross, the theme should not stand out too strongly (p. 69).

As stated by the translator of that publication, Richard Zimdars, the only obvious instance of hand-crossing is present in the above-mentioned measures of Consolation 4. Therefore, one could conclude that those measures could be performed either way. However, the original notation suggests crossed hands; playing the theme with left hand will bring out a slightly different sonority, since thumb will be used for the upper part of the melody, and not 3–4–5 as in the beginning. This edition includes an alternate fingering, in the case that playing with crossed hands becomes too much of a stretch.

Consolation No. 5

The first version of this work is dated 1844, and was titled Madrigal. With this piece, the cycle returns to the original key of E Major. The fingering suggested in this edition was carefully selected to bring out the correct articulation of this beautiful song-like piece.

Consolation No. 6

The longest and most difficult piece in this set, this piece requires well-developed chordal control. The choice of tempo is important: it should be fast enough for the correct feeling of Allegretto, while keeping the big chordal texture under control and not too agitated. The quasi cadenza in m. 68 should be played with brilliance, bringing the main theme back in a culminating way. The coda returns to the quiet mood that overall permeates this cycle, ending it in E Major, in the low register of the instrument.

Drei Liebesträume: Drei Notturnos

According with the comprehensive list of works available in the *New Grove Dictionary of Music and Musicians*, the Drei Liebesträume (Drei Notturnos) were published in Lepzig in 1850 and were not composed in the order they are now known. Liszt's Liebesträume were first published for high voice and piano, and later adapted for solo piano. In the original songs, Liszt used poems by the German poets Ludwig Uhland (1787–1862, Liebesträume Nos. 1 and 2) and Ferdinand Freiligrath (1810–1876, Liebestraum No. 3).

The most famous of the three pieces, Liebestraum No. 3, was the first to be composed and is often referred to as "the" Liebestraum. This song was composed in 1843, while the second ("Gestorben war ich") was started in 1845, and the first piece in the set ("Hohe Liebe") was probably composed in 1850. The reason for the inverted chronological order is not clear.

Liszt enjoyed the task of transcribing songs for solo piano, a fact proven by the many such arrangements he did of songs by Schubert, Schumann and several other composers. His own original songs, composed and published in 1843 (Buch der Lieder), were arranged for solo piano soon after their publication. What sets the transcriptions of the Liebesträume apart from their original versions is the fact that Liszt added the subtitle Drei Notturnos. Starting with John Field and taken to perfection by Frederic Chopin, the genre of the Nocturne became almost synonymous with slow, quiet, romantic piano pieces. By adding the subtitle, one could argue that Liszt was calling attention to these pieces as "real" piano works, not simply transcriptions to be performed by pianists only when a singer was not available.

The second Notturno, in its original, simplified form, became the first piece of a five-piece set composed for Olga von Meyendorff, and is published in this edition as an appendix.

The autograph of the three Liebesträume is located in a private collection and unavailable for consultation. This edition is based on the 1850 first edition and its reissue in 1886, as published in 1998 by Henle Edition (Ernst-Günter Heinemann and Klaus Schilde, editors). Other editions consulted are: Editio Musica Budapest (1982, Imre Sulyok and Imre Mezo, editors), Ricordi (E. R. 843, Ettore Pozzoli, editor, date unknown), Schirmer (Schirmer's Library of Musical Classics, vol. 341, 1895/1915, Rafael Joseffy, editor), Wood (no. 315, 1904, John Preston, editor) and PWM Edition (Polskie Wydawnictwo Muzyczne, 1986, Stanislaw Szpinalski, editor). Minor inconsistencies between the editions are indicated with footnotes.

Liebestraum (Notturno) No. 1: Hohe Liebe

In the same key of its famous counterpart, this piece definitely needs to be performed more often. In fact, it is worth noticing that this was one of the three works Liszt chose to perform in his very last public appearance, in Luxembourg, on July 19, 1886, twelve days before his death. According to Alan Walker, that evening in Luxembourg

> was not only the last time that Liszt played in public, but it may also have been the last time he ever touched the keys of a piano. With these three pieces, ["Hohe Liebe," one of his arrangements of Chopin's Chants Polonais and the sixth of his *Soirées de Vienne*] as La Mara later expressed, Liszt's magical playing fell silent for ever (Walker, *The Final Years*, p. 506).

Liszt uses a very soft dynamic (*una corda*), creating the necessary mood for the melody to blossom. As a rule, the melody should be played with arm weight, to differentiate it from the accompaniment figurations. The trill section (mm. 67–75) can be played either in a measured or unmeasured way. Liszt used to ask his students to play it as fast as possible, but keep in mind that an even and gentle trill will sound great as well. Starting the trill with the upper note will make it much simpler to perform.

Liebestraum (Notturno) No. 2: Seliger Tod

The sharpness of E Major is enhanced by its positioning between Nos. 1 and 3, both set in the warm key of A-flat Major. Because of that and the poetry that inspired it, this Notturno is much more declamatory and dramatic. After a dreamy, unsettled introduction, the song starts solo, punctuated by accompanying chords (*il canto accentuato assai*). All efforts should be made to keep a considerable difference in color between the melody and the chords. The same theme becomes more fluid in the second verse (*dolcissimo armonioso*, mm. 35–43) and requires the use of cross-hand technique.

Liebestraum (Notturno) No. 3: O Lieb

This piece requires no introduction—it is one of the most famous pieces in the piano repertoire. This piece offers several possibilities for expressive playing in different pianistic textures: melody in the middle register, surrounded by bass and accompaniment (mm. 1–23), and melody on top (mm. 26–37), melody accompanied by arpeggios (mm. 37–58), melody on top accompanied by crossed-hand chords (mm. 61–68). In all textures, the melody should have a very distinctive sound and color, never being mixed in the accompaniment. These sections are interpolated by effective cadenzas, creating a very satisfying and pianistic work.

Bibliography

Jerger, Wilhelm, ed. "The Piano Masterclasses of Franz Liszt, 1884–1886." *Diary Notes of August Göllerich*. Translated and enlarged by Richard Louis Zimdars. Indiana University Press: Bloomington, Indiana, 1996.

Ramann, Lina. *Liszt-Pädagogium: Klavier-Kompositionen Franz Liszts nebst noch unedirten Veränderungen, Zusätzen und Kadenzen nach des Meisters Lehren pädagogisch glossirt von Lina Ramann.* Leipzig, 1901. As quoted in EMB, Z. 12 697.

Searle, Humphrey. *The Music of Liszt.* Dover Publications: New York, NY 1966.

Walker, Alan. *Franz Liszt: The Final Years, 1861–1886.* Cornell University Press: Ithaca, New York, 1996.

Walker, Alan. *Franz Liszt: The Weimar Years, 1848–1861.* Cornell University Press: Ithaca, New York, 1989.

CD Credits

Lance Miller, Recording Engineer
Alexandre Dossin, Producer and Pianist
Recorded at Aasen-Hull Hall, University of Oregon School of Music and Dance

Consolations

1.

Franz Liszt

Andante con moto [♩ = 92–100]

2.

Un poco più mosso [♩ = 116–126]

13

14

3.

4.

5.

*Some editions print D-sharp instead of E.
**Some editions print B instead of D-sharp.

6.

Allegretto sempre cantabile [♩. = 56–60]

LIEBESTRAUM NO. 1

Hohe Liebe

Von Ludwig Uhland

In Liebesarmen ruht ihr trunken,
Des Lebens Früchte winken euch;
Ein Blick nur ist auf mich gesunken,
Doch bin ich vor euch allen reich.

Das Glück der Erde miss' ich gerne
Und blick', ein Märtyrer, hinan,
Denn über mir in goldner Ferne
Hat sich der Himmel aufgetan.

Exalted Love

By Ludwig Uhland

In love's embrace, entranced and dreaming,
To you the fruits of earth seem fair;
And yet, one glance upon me gleaming
Has made me rich beyond compare.

Forsaking every idle pleasure,
As martyrs in the days of old,
The golden sky my soul can measure
And heavenly mysteries unfold.

Translation by Anna Mathewson

Liebesträume
Three Nocturnes for Piano

1.

Franz Liszt

Andantino espressivo assai [♩ = 84–92]

il canto accentuato assai

dolcissimo

una corda

*l'accompagnamento sempre **pp** e colla parte*

smorz.

ppp

*Taking the Es with the left hand should be used only when hands are too small to reach a 7th or a 9th.

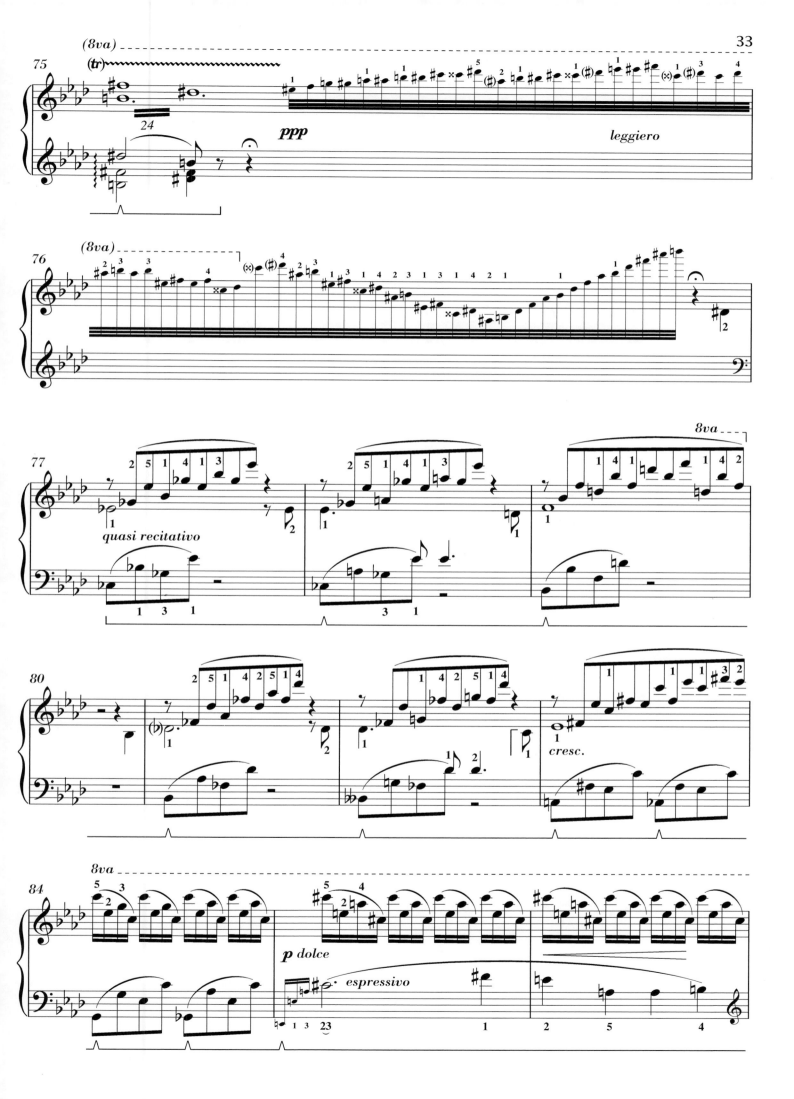

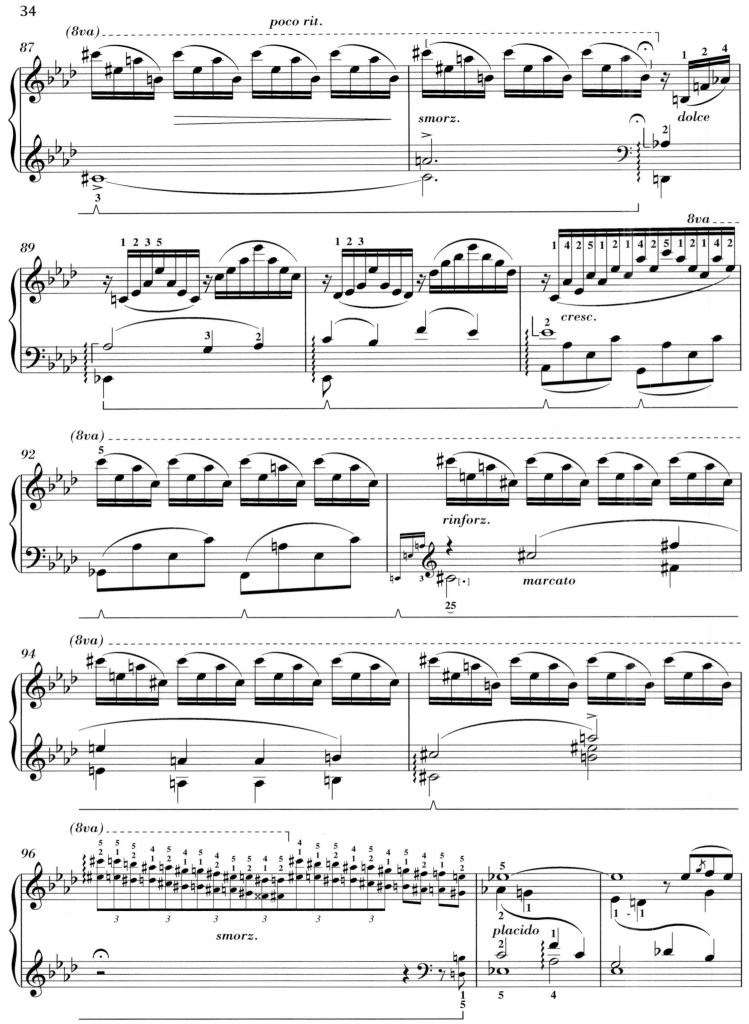

LIEBESTRAUM NO. 2

Seliger Tod

Von Ludwig Uhland
Gestorben war ich
Vor Liebeswonn';
Begraben lag ich
In ihren Armen;
Erwecket ward ich
Von ihren Küssen,
Den Himmel sah ich
In ihren Augen.

Happy Death

By Ludwig Uhland
All lifeless was I,
By love o'erpowered;
All buried was I
In embraces tender;
Awakened was I
When kisses showered,
And within your eyes
Saw Heaven's splendor.

Translation by Anna Mathewson

2.

Quasi lento, abbandonandosi [♩ = 69–76]

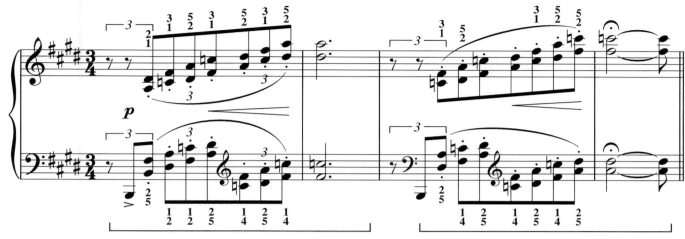

il canto accentuato assai

★Press the key without allowing the hammer to strike, and change pedal.

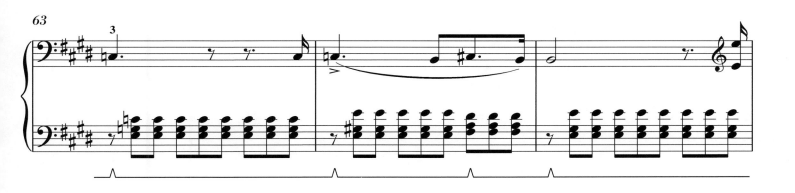

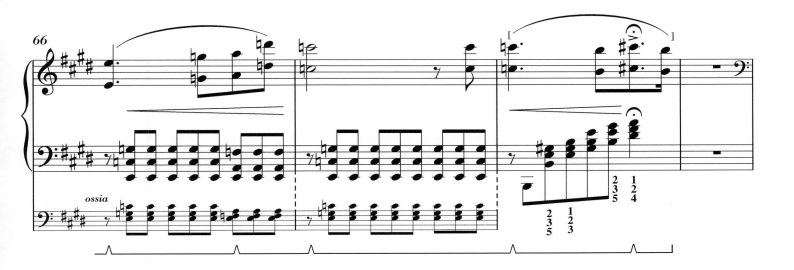

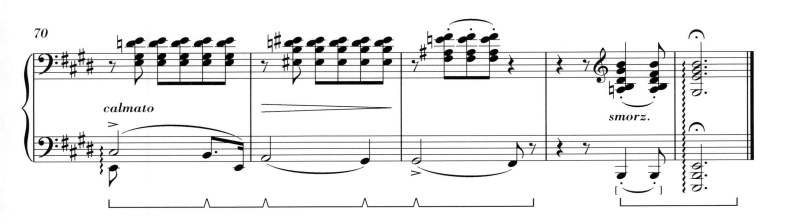

LIEBESTRAUM NO. 3

O Lieb

Von Ferdinand Freiligrath

O Lieb', o lieb' so lang du lieben kannst, so lang du lieben magst,

Die Stunde kommt, wo du an Gräbern stehst und klagst

Und sorge, dass dein Herze glüht, und Liebe hegt und Liebe trägt,

So lang ihm noch ein ander Herz in Liebe warm entgegenschlägt.

Und wer dir seine Brust erschliesst, o thu' ihm, was du kannst zu lieb',

Und mach' ihm jede Stunde froh, und mach ihm keine Stunde trüb!

Und hüte deine Zunge wohl; bald ist ein hartes Wort entfloh'n.

O Gott—es war nicht bös gemeint—der Andere aber geht und weint.

O Love

By Ferdinand Freiligrath

O love while thou hast yet the power! O love while love is near at hand!

Ere dawns a day when by the grave thou mayst in lonely sorrow stand.

Prepare within thy heart a home where love is sheltered and at rest,

And where another yearning heart may enter as a welcome guest.

And whosoever unto thee his inmost soul in trust doth show,

For love's sweet sake bestow some boon, nor add unto his weight of woe.

Guard weel thy lips, lest cruel words should slip beyond, and thou shalt say:

"O God, I meant no wrong!" Too late! The loved one, weeping, goes away.

Translation by Anna Mathewson

3.

Poco allegro, con affetto [♩ = 126–132]

*Some editions print D-flat instead of B-flat.

*Some editions print octave D-flats.

*Some editions print B-flat instead of G.
**Some editions print D-natural; likely an error.

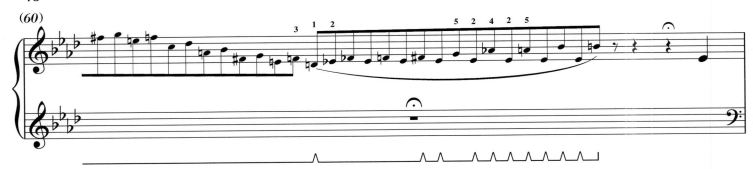

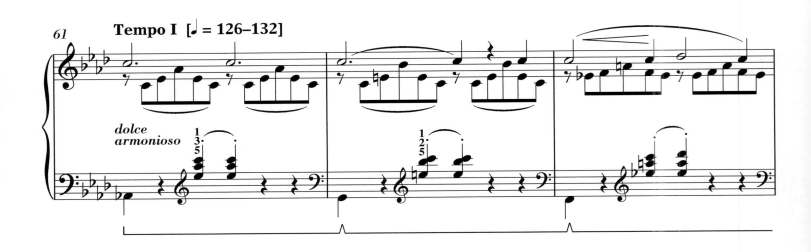

Tempo I [♩ = 126–132]

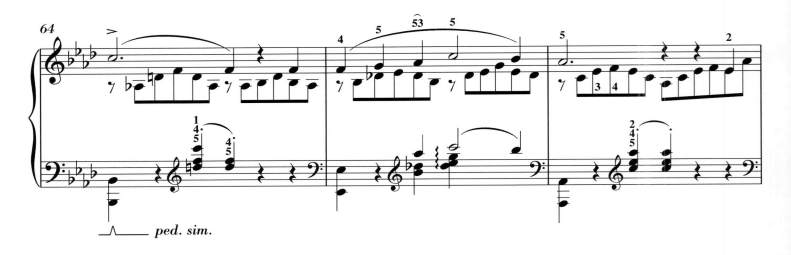

APPENDIX

Liebestraum No. 2
Original Version

Franz Liszt

Lento espressivo

ABOUT THE EDITOR

ALEXANDRE DOSSIN

Considered by Martha Argerich an "extraordinary musician" and by international critics a "phenomenon" and "a master of contrasts," Alexandre Dossin keeps active performing, recording, and teaching careers.

Born in Brazil, where he lived until he was nineteen, Dossin spent nine years studying in Moscow, Russia, before establishing residency in the United States. This background allows him to be fluent in several languages and equally comfortable in a wide range of piano repertoire.

Currently on the faculty of the University of Oregon School of Music, Dossin is a graduate from the University of Texas-Austin and the Moscow Tchaikovsky Conservatory in Russia. He studied with and was an assistant of Sergei Dorensky at the Tchaikovsky Conservatory, and William Race and Gregory Allen at UT-Austin.

A prizewinner in several international piano competitions, Dossin received the First Prize and the Special Prize at the 2003 Martha Argerich International Piano Competition in Buenos Aires, Argentina. Other awards include the Silver Medal and Second Honorable Mention in the Maria Callas Grand Prix and Third Prize and Special Prize in the Mozart International Piano Competition.

He performed numerous live recitals for public radio in Texas, Wisconsin, and Illinois, including returning engagements at the Dame Myra Hess Memorial Concert Series. Dossin has performed in over twenty countries, including international festivals in Japan, Canada, the United States, Brazil, and Argentina, on some occasions sharing the stage with Martha Argerich. He was a soloist with the Brazilian Symphony, Buenos Aires Philharmonic, Mozarteum Symphony, and São Paulo Symphony, having collaborated with renowned conductors such as Charles Dutoit, Michael Gielen, Isaac Karabtchevsky, Keith Clark, and Eleazar de Carvalho.

Dossin has CDs released by Musicians Showcase Recording (2002), Blue Griffin (*A Touch of Brazil*, 2005), and Naxos (*Verdi-Liszt Paraphrases*, 2007; *Kabalevsky Complete Sonatas and Sonatinas*, 2009; *Kabalevsky Complete Preludes*, 2009; *Liszt in Russia*, 2011), praised in reviews by *Diapason*, *The Financial Times*, *Fanfare Magazine*, *American Record Guide*, *Clavier* and other international publications.

In the United States, Alexandre Dossin was featured as the main interview and on the cover of *Clavier* magazine and interviewed by *International Piano Magazine* (South Korea). He is an editor and recording artist for several Schirmer Performance Editions.

Dossin is a member of the Board of Directors for the American Liszt Society and the President of the Oregon Chapter of the American Liszt Society. He lives in the beautiful south hills of Eugene with his wife Maria, and children Sophia and Victor.
www.dossin.net